BE A FLAMINGO

& stand out from the crowd

BE A FLAMINGO

& stand out from the crowd

SARAH FORD

ILLUSTRATED BY
ANITA MANGAN

spruce

NOTES

 This book contains nuttiness.

 Not for the moaning kind.

 Rated PG (good for pigeon guidance).

 Add extra spice of life to enhance flavour.

 Spread the pink.

Be a flamingo. Flamingo is one of a kind; utterly unforgettable, he is charming, compassionate and fabulous. Flamingo embraces his feminine side, but there's more to these pink feathers than meets the eye, so beware when he flashes the black ones, as he's no pushover and always retains the element of surprise.

There's always method in Flamingo's madness. He is climbing the palm tree to success, taking some risks along the way, but, fear not, he will never trample over anyone else to get there. His dogged determination to see things through and his creative approach to problem-solving are what make him special. He'll be the first to volunteer (there's always something good in even the most boring task), he always tries to embrace change (yum, crispy squid with seaweed for tea), and his manners are extolled from South America to Africa (they are yet to find out about his wind problem).

You'll never find Flamingo sat in front of a sitcom; he's too busy cooking from scratch, learning Mandarin or doing the open mic at his local comedy club.

Flamingo has never felt the need to fit in. He likes himself, he is happy in his own feathers and doesn't care what anyone else thinks, and that is what makes him one of the best.

FLAMINGO'S 10 RULES FOR A GOOD LIFE

- Be creative... open your eyes and take inspiration from everything and everyone around you (even pigeons look quite cute in the right light).

- Go for it, go the extra mile, offer a helping hand or stay late to get the job done (much better than watching a box set back to back).

- Be curious and master the art of conversation (if in doubt, ask lots of questions, then you've ticked both boxes).

- See the funny side; a sense of humour will get you through the toughest times and will also guarantee you'll always have friends, even if your jokes are rubbish.

- Dress to impress, chuck fashion out the window and find your own style, but don't forget the importance of matching socks.
- Choose your own path. It might be rocky or where the dog-walkers have gone before, but it's yours and it's more likely to lead you to a good place.
- Embrace imperfection – it's so much more interesting.
- Take a risk – it might just pay off.
- Start small... good morning greetings, a genuine compliment or wearing a hat and soon the small stuff will turn into the memorable big stuff.
- Grasp opportunity and embrace change. Seize the day, don't be the one who wished they had.

Flamingo pondered for
a moment whether his
legs looked thin in these,
but wore them anyway.

Flamingo was ready to embrace the unknown.

Today, Flamingo
was going to be his
own cheerleader.

Flamingo never felt the
need to follow the crowd.

Flamingo liked to pay
attention to detail,
especially when
choosing his socks.

Today, Flamingo
was practising his
festival eyes.

It's true, thought
Flamingo, money
does not buy style.

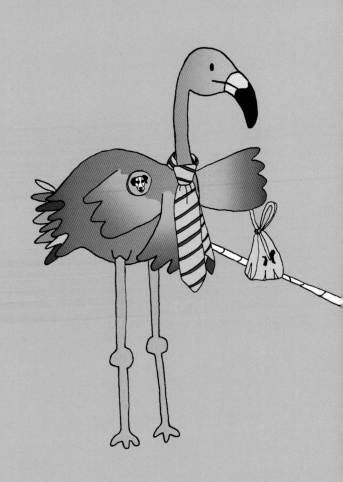

Flamingo had accessorized
beautifully but now this was
going to ruin it all.

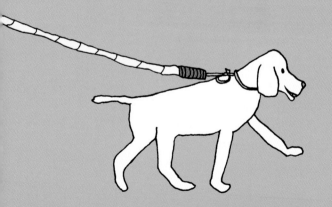

Flamingo was a creature of moderation... he would only eat the broken cookies.

Flamingo was as fresh as
a daisy after a good sleep
on his downy pillow.

Flamingo never felt
fully dressed without
a winning smile.

Flamingo always stood up
to make his sales calls.

He had only had two
Negronis but was
feeling on top of his
game; three, and it
would be all over.

To be kind, Flamingo
sometimes pretended
to be interested.

Even if he won big on
the lottery, Flamingo
wouldn't change a thing.

Flamingo had chosen
his friends wisely.

Flamingo had practised maintaining eye contact and was a master of the blink game.

Flamingo was writing
his thank-you notes.

All the hard work had
paid off; his shoes
definitely outshone
the rest.

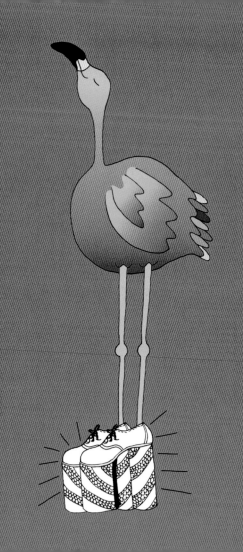

He was never boastful,
but occasionally Flamingo
would give his trumpet
a small toot.

Flamingo had a policy
of saying yes.

Credit where credit's due,
thought Flamingo, Penguin
knew how to put on a show.

Flamingo was pleased
with his photobomb.

Flamingo thought no
hurdle was too big.

Don't ask, don't get,
thought Flamingo.

Flamingo knew that
sometimes ruffling
feathers was for the
greater good.

A grand entrance called for
Flamingo's statement piece.

Flamingo was not afraid of failure, apart from when he was going parachuting.

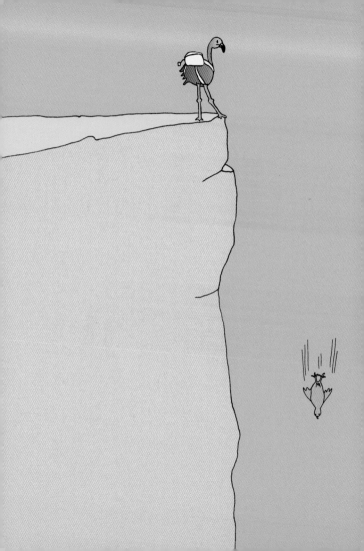

In order to give his
outfit a lift, Flamingo
had added a scarf.

It was a difficult situation,
but Flamingo faced up to
it with his shoulders back
and his head high.

Flamingo thought that no one looked good in leggings.

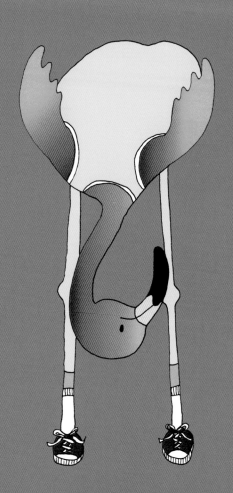

Flamingo liked to
cause a ripple.

UGH,
STINKY!

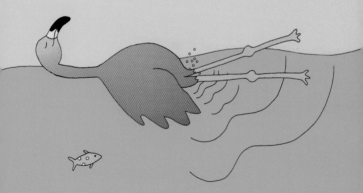

When something extra was needed, Flamingo deployed the black feathers.

Flamingo thought it
was win-win when
it came to tickling.

Flamingo had an
extra helping of
shrimps so that he
would look extra pink
for his dating profile.

Flamingo tried hard to
remember everyone's name.

HELLO,
I'M FLAMINGO.
PLEASED TO
MEET YOU.

Good manners are
always in fashion,
thought Flamingo.

Flamingo was always
the first to volunteer.

It is good to be generous,
thought Flamingo.

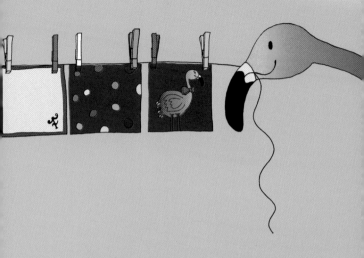

Flamingo never went
anywhere without his
handkerchief.

Flamingo was comfortable
with who he was.

Much as he loved his tablet, Flamingo thought it was better to really connect.

Flamingo was embracing
his pinkness.

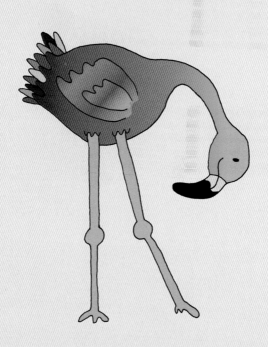

Flamingo was thinking
outside the box. Now
be a flamingo and do
the same.

An Hachette UK Company
www.hachette.co.uk

First published in Great Britain
in 2017 by Spruce, a division of
Octopus Publishing Group Ltd
Carmelite House
50 Victoria Embankment
London EC4Y 0DZ
www.octopusbooks.co.uk

Copyright © Octopus Publishing
Group 2017
Text copyright © Sarah Ford 2017
Illustrations copyright © Anita
Mangan 2017

Distributed in the US by
Hachette Book Group
1290 Avenue of the Americas
4th and 5th Floors
New York, NY 10104

Distributed in Canada by
Canadian Manda Group
664 Annette St.
Toronto, Ontario, Canada M6S 2C8

Sarah Ford asserts the moral right
to be identified as the author of
this work.

ISBN 978-1-84601-554-0

A CIP catalogue record for this
book is available from the British
Library.

Printed and bound in China

10 9 8 7 6 5 4 3 2

Commissioning Editor
Sarah Ford

Editorial Assistant
Ellie Corbett

Designer and Illustrator
Anita Mangan

Senior Designer
Jaz Bahra

Production Controller
Sarah Kulasek-Boyd

Proofreader
Helen Ridge